DIVERSITY MOSAIC PARTICIPANT WORKBOOK

LEADING DIVERSITY

Tina Rasmussen, Ph.D.

Pfeiffer
A Wiley Imprint
www.pfeiffer.com

Published by Pfeiffer
An Imprint of Wiley
One Montgomery, Ste. 1200, San Francisco, CA 94104
www.pfeiffer.com

For additional copies/bulk purchases of this book in the U.S. please contact 800-274-4434.

Pfeiffer books and products are available through most bookstores. To contact Pfeiffer directly call our Customer Care Department within the U.S. at 800-274-4434, outside the U.S. at 317-572-3985, fax 317-572-4002, or visit www.pfeiffer.com.

Pfeiffer also publishes its books in a variety of electronic formats. Some content that appears in print may not be available in electronic books.

ISBN-13: 978-0-7879-8173-0

Acquiring Editor: Matthew Davis
Director of Development: Kathleen Dolan Davies
Developmental Editor: Susan Rachmeler
Production Editor: Dawn Kilgore
Editor: Rebecca Taff
Manufacturing Supervisor: Becky Carreño

Printing   10   9   8   7   6   5   4   3   2

Contents

Overview and Objectives

WELCOME! *Diversity Mosaic: Leading Diversity* is designed to help people who manage others and set policy at all levels (executives, middle managers, supervisors, group leads, and board members) to develop knowledge, awareness, and skills required by leaders in creating a truly inclusive organization. It will also help you understand what the organization expects of leaders in supporting the organization's diversity initiative.

When you have completed the workshop you will:

- Understand leaders' unique roles in creating a successful diversity initiative *(knowledge)*

- Understand why cultural competence is important for us as leaders *(knowledge)*

- Understand the concept of structural inequality and leaders' role in addressing it *(knowledge)*

- Analyze our perceptions, strengths, and development areas in leading diversity *(awareness)*

- Learn skills to increase our level of cultural competence as leaders *(skill)*

- Determine how to demonstrate support for the organization's diversity and inclusion effort by developing our ability to communicate the Cornerstone concepts effectively *(skill)*

- Create a personal action plan for leading diversity and creating true inclusion in the workplace *(knowledge, awareness, skill)*

The *Cultural Mosaic: Leading Diversity* workshop agenda is comprised of three sections. Your facilitator will have more detailed information on the agenda when you arrive at the session. Following is the agenda:

- Diversity Mosaic Review

- Leading Diversity

- Creating True Inclusion

Pages 33 through 63 of this workbook contain all the forms required for you to complete a 360-degree assessment. This process will enable you to gain insight into how others perceive your behavior with regard to leading diversity and creating an inclusive environment. Feel free to read this entire workbook (as well as the 360-degree feedback section) at any time to understand more about leading diversity and prepare yourself for the assessment and the workshop. Your facilitator will let you know whether you should complete the 360-degree assessment before the session, or whether you are to wait until the session to receive further instructions before completing it.

Cornerstone 1: The Inclusive Definition of Diversity

Diversity

is the mosaic of people
who bring a variety of
backgrounds, styles, perspectives, beliefs and competencies
as assets to the groups and organizations
with whom they interact.

Dimensions of Diversity

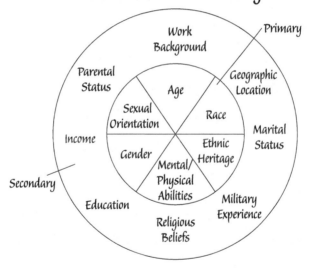

Cultural Competence

is a set of competencies and skills
that individuals and organizations can use
to create a truly inclusive environment
that values diversity.

Cornerstone 2: The Business Case for Diversity

THE BUSINESS CASE IS one of the foundational starting points of our diversity initiative, because it answers the question "Why are we doing this?" There are many solid business reasons why our organization is making diversity and inclusion one of our top strategic business considerations. Which of the reasons below seem the most pressing to you?

We need to be true to our mission.

- ☐ We want to live our organization's mission and values.
- ☐ To accomplish our mission, we must show authentic positive regard for everyone who touches our organization.
- ☐ It's the next step in the evolution of our organization.
- ☐ We would like our organization to be a role model of inclusion to other organizations.
- ☐ We are required by our organizational bylaws to refrain from discrimination.

We want to expand who uses our services by becoming more inclusive of all people.

- ☐ We need to learn about more of our customers' needs.
- ☐ We can't serve groups we have unconscious biases against—or even those we just fail to understand.
- ☐ We need to reach customers and/or volunteers/donors we may currently be missing.
- ☐ Research shows that worker satisfaction is the number one predictor of customer satisfaction. If our employees feel valued, they'll treat the people we serve well.
- ☐ Valuing diversity and being inclusive can help us revitalize our organization.
- ☐ Recruiting a diverse board will increase awareness of customer needs and opportunities.

We need to proactively address social/demographic trends to remain viable.

- ☐ Diversity has been one of the largest trends in corporations for many years. We need to catch up.
- ☐ Other organizations are addressing diversity; we can't slip behind.
- ☐ Being known for diversity attracts customers/donors. Diversity is often required for funding.

We need to maximize employee potential and productivity.

☐   Workplace demographics have shifted more in the last twenty years than in the previous one hundred years. We need to adjust to remain current with societal trends.

☐   We are short on employees/volunteers. We need to attract applicants from wider talent pools.

☐   We have a hard time attracting non-traditional candidates, and we want to improve at this.

☐   It costs $10,000 or more to fill a vacated job. Valuing diversity can reduce our turnover.

☐   Community good will for valuing diversity can open doors and attract employees/customers.

☐   Valuing people increases their "discretionary contribution." We want to maximize productivity.

☐   We'd like to have more synergy and creativity. Differences provide the ingredients for this.

☐   We want to improve decision making and engage diverse views to help overcome "groupthink."

☐   We need to more quickly integrate people into the organization (mergers, transfers, new hires, etc.).

☐   As people retire, we need to find ways to transfer their intellectual capital to others.

☐   Our morale, employee surveys, and/or exit interviews have indicated possible diversity problems.

We need to prevent tarnish to our reputation and enhance our public image.

☐   Organizations have been sued when they didn't value diversity. We don't want that to happen.

☐   We don't want to discourage customers/donors by having a reputation for excluding people.

☐   We want to avoid blunders that occur when a variety of perspectives is absent.

We need to remain effective as leaders.

☐   Cultural competence is a minimum requirement for the effective leader of today. We need to ensure we're up-to-date on the facts and know how to address potential issues.

☐   Leaders need to be role models. We want to raise our skills before asking others to do so.

☐   People are often unaware of offending others. Gaining cultural competence is an opportunity to grow personally by "seeing our own lenses."

Add your own: _____

_____

_____

_____

_____

_____

Cornerstone 5: The Diversity Enhancement Process

Step 1—Why do this? Board/CEO and senior leaders commit to undertaking long-term action.
Output: Diversity Initiative Chart of Work; Team Formed

Step 6—How far did we get? Diversity team measures progress on goals against baselines. Board/CEO and senior leaders reward successes and use data on improvement areas to create new plan. (Cycle repeats.)
Output: Published Results, People/Teams Rewarded

Step 2—Where are we? Diversity team gathers information to discover apparent as well as underlying issues. Findings establish quantitative and qualitative baselines to measure future progress.
Output: Diversity Assessment Results—Strengths, Obstacles, and Key Issues

Step 1:
Board/CEO
Initiates

Step 2:
Assess/
Step 6:
Reassess
and Reward

Step 5:
Mobilize
Commitment
to Implement,
Adjust

Step 3:
Create Vision,
Goals, Plan,
Budget

Step 4:
Design
Improvement
Processes

Step 3—Where do we want to go? Board/CEO and senior leaders create vision with goals and success measures. Diversity team develops plan to accomplish them.
Output: Vision, Success Measures, Action Plan, Budget

Step 5—Who's coming with us? Leaders and diversity team mobilize people's commitment to implement improvements. People make adjustments as needed.
Output: A "critical mass" of energized people who take action

Step 4—How do we get there? Diversity team designs improvement processes that will achieve goals according to plan.
Output: Improvement Processes (Communication, Awareness and Skills development, Board/Leader Development, Recruiting, and Retention)

Cornerstone 3: The Cultural Competence Scorecard

HISTORICALLY, measures of success at diversity focused almost solely on increasing the number of non-traditional employees in certain jobs (i.e., more women and people of color). This approach may have produced more "diversity," but failed to address the climate considerations needed for success. It also created "us versus them" divisions. The Cultural Competence Scorecard below lists three types of measures, two of which emphasize creating a culture of inclusion and enhancing the organization's reputation and one of which focuses on improving specific demographic profiles.

The Cultural Competence Scorecard

Workplace Culture
▣ How inclusive is our internal environment?

Marketplace Reputation
▣ How inclusive do people outside our organization perceive us to be?

Representation
▣ To what extent do our people reflect the communities we serve?

Workplace Culture + Reputation ➤ Representation

The historical situation regarding how diversity was addressed can be likened to stocking and maintaining a fish tank. Traditional diversity efforts that focused solely on hiring and training were about "putting new fish into the water" or "teaching the fish to be nice to each other." While these efforts can produce some valuable benefits, they are not likely to create long-term systemic change. Why? Because they overlook the fact that the water in the tank is polluted! And they expect the new fish to clean the water. We must look directly at the water to be successful at inclusion. If we don't, the new fish will eventually jump out of the tank, and some of the existing fish might, too. Or the fish might get sick from toxicity. The problem is that we're the fish, and it's difficult to see the water because it's all around us! Only when the water is fresh and clean are fish able to be healthy and productive in it.

The Cultural Competence Scorecard shows us that we must measure the internal environment *first*. Only when "the water" is sure to be healthy for everyone can we start to work on our reputation—how people outside see us. If we truly have an inclusive organization, we can then start talking about it, which will attract a wide variety of people to want to work here, buy our products and services, partner with us by contractual agreements, or buy our stock. When our environment is inclusive *and* people know about it, then representation is a natural outcome. The key is that representation is an *outcome,* not a cause! Historically, people thought putting in "new fish" (representation) would *cause* the environment to change. In reality, we need to be inclusive and welcoming ourselves for diversity and inclusion to last.

Leading Diversity Versus Traditional Management

Traditional Management

The effective and efficient utilization of employees in pursuit of the organization's mission, goals, and objectives is what we mean by traditional management.

Leading Diversity

Leading diversity is a comprehensive management process that addresses the organization's infrastructures to create an environment that enables *all* members of a workforce to be productive, without advantaging or disadvantaging *anyone* (Dr. R. Roosevelt Thomas, *Harvard Business Review,* 1990). Leading diversity has two components:

- As an individual—setting a tone for inclusion
- As a power in the infrastructure—eliminating structural inequality

Of course, leaders must set a tone for inclusion by being role models, because others will follow what the leader *does* rather than what he or she *says*. But leading diversity also means understanding how—as leaders—we have been entrusted with the power to affect the *infrastructures* that make the organization run. Leaders must recognize and correct instances of structural inequality that require solutions beyond the interpersonal need to be "nicer" to each other. Examples of organizational infrastructures the leader is responsible for include mission, strategies, goals, information sharing, and employment processes (recruiting/selection, compensation, rewards, promotions, performance management), all of which serve to create the organizational culture.

Questions

How is leading diversity different from traditional management?

What additional skills may be required for leading diversity?

Why might leaders avoid, overlook, or resist leading diversity?

What do leaders have to gain by becoming good at leading diversity?

Cornerstone 4: The Diversity Adoption Curve

AS WITH ANY CHANGE, the move to valuing diversity is an ongoing process that evolves over time. Even so, we sometimes expect that if people attend a diversity workshop, the change should automatically follow. Here's an analogy. What percentage of people do you think are aware of how to eat healthfully? Now, what percentage do you think actually eat healthfully? Why doesn't everyone eat healthfully, since most people know of the positive benefits? Many factors contribute, but two primary ones are *habit* and *conditioning*. Increasing our knowledge is only a first step—changing our behavior requires much more effort.

One of the best summaries of this concept of change (see diagram below) comes from Marilyn Loden's second book, *Implementing Diversity*. We do not *create* the Diversity Adoption Curve; it occurs naturally. Knowing about it can help us understand how change happens. This process has been discovered over and over in behavioral science research on many different types of change.

The Leading Diversity Assessment, found later in this workbook, can help you assess your own location on the curve. Your facilitator will have more information about how to use the assessment, either before or during the workshop.

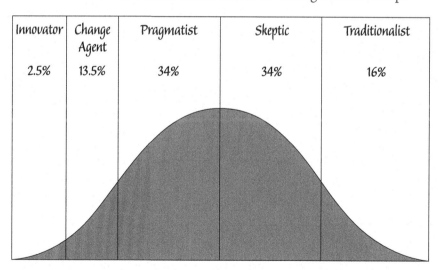

Innovator	Change Agent	Pragmatist	Skeptic	Traditionalist
2.5%	13.5%	34%	34%	16%

Increased Perceived Opportunity   Decreased Perceived Opportunity

←————————————————————————→

Decreased Perceived Risk   Increased Perceived Risk

Adapted from *Implementing Diversity* by Marilyn Loden. Copyright © 1996 by McGraw-Hill. Reproduced with permission of The McGraw-Hill Companies.

How Leaders Set a Tone for Inclusion

SETTING THE TONE for inclusion is the *single most important* thing one can do in leading diversity. Leaders must value diversity themselves and model the skills for others. People notice when a leader is willing to admit that he or she isn't perfect when it comes to diversity and is willing to learn and stretch out of his or her "comfort zone" just like everyone else. When leaders are aware of people's uniqueness and show appreciation for it, team members notice and begin to emulate the behavior. Leaders set a tone for inclusion in one or more of three ways.

Be a Role Model

If behavior that is in direct opposition to valuing diversity is allowed to go uncorrected, people will get the message that the whole initiative is just "lip service." Leaders must have the courage to "walk their talk" for change to occur. Obtaining feedback from others through 360-degree feedback is an excellent way for us to gain insight on how others perceive our behavior and on the impact it is having on the overall work climate of our groups and organizations.

Use the Platinum Rule

"Treating others as *they* want to be treated" is especially important for managers. In attempting to lead diversity using a "one-size-fits-all" approach, leaders can unintentionally project their own backgrounds, perceptions, and beliefs onto others whose needs are dramatically different. The "treat-everyone-the-same" approach became popular historically as an effort to eliminate discriminatory treatment of nontraditional employees. But people are not all the same. Using one standard system that fits the leader will limit the productivity of the employees. It is now widely accepted that this approach is less effective than one in which leaders tailor their style to each employee—by employing The Platinum Rule—"Treat others as *they* want to be treated."

Project Positive Self-Fulfilling Prophecies

Research has shown that we tend to see people as we *expect* to see them, regardless of their actual *behavior*. This is also known as *The Pygmalion Effect*, from a book of the same name. The first time this was noted, in 1969, Harvard University conducted a study in which elementary school teachers were told that 205 of their students were "intellectual bloomers," but that they were not to treat them any differently from the other students. In reality, the students had been picked at random and had average IQs. At the end of the study, the "bloomers" showed intelligence gains much higher than those of their classmates, due to special treatment by the teachers. Similar studies were conducted with welders and office workers. The implications of the self-fulfilling prophecy in the workplace are dramatic, because leaders are in the position to be able to authorize or to extend or withhold rewards.

If we assume people will fail, they often do—largely as a result of our expectations. The opposite is true as well. As leaders, wouldn't we rather enter the situation with the assumption that people *are* competent and *will* succeed, until we see otherwise? The self-fulfilling prophecy is especially important with nontraditional employees because the traditional work environment has automatically viewed them as less competent, putting them at an immediate disadvantage.

Leader/Team Member Discussion Questions

1. What do you want most from your job?

2. Under what conditions do you do your best work?

3. How would you like me to show recognition of your hard work?

4. How do you want to be rewarded?

5. How would you like to receive suggestions for improving your work?

6. What are your short-term career goals?

7. What are your longer-term career goals?

8. How can I help you reach your career goals?

9. In what ways do you think people on our team, including yourself, are different from one another? In what ways are we similar?

10. How do our differences affect our working together as a team?

11. How do these differences affect interpersonal relationships on the job?

12. How do these differences affect our overall productivity?

13. What things am I doing that help the team work together?

14. What do I do that might be hurting our productivity?

15. What suggestions do you have for me as the team leader?

16. What biases do you perceive that I have?

17. How do these biases manifest themselves in my actions?

18. What policies or procedures inhibit your best work?

19. Is there anything else you'd like to tell me or ask me that we haven't talked about?

Creating Structural Equality

PEOPLE WITH THE AUTHORITY to select, reward, promote, and terminate others need to be aware of the many opportunities for structural inequality in the employment process, and they must take steps to ensure that these infrastructures are equal for all employees. Four of the most important of these infrastructures are

- Recruiting
- Retention
- Team Leadership
- Communication

Recruiting

The most obvious sign that a company has begun to value diversity is when nontraditional employees are actively recruited, selected, and promoted into positions of authority. The goal of any recruitment, selection, or promotion efforts is to find the candidate who can best fulfill the responsibilities of the job. The purpose of interviewing, then, is to determine to what degree the applicant is capable of fulfilling the requirements of the job. The purpose is *not* to determine whether the person is *similar to* the person he or she is replacing, whether the person is similar to *the interviewer,* or to find out whether we have anything in common with the person.

Recruiting is an area in which the structural blocks to valuing diversity become obvious. Often, well-intentioned leaders report that they "couldn't find any non-traditional candidates" and that they "just aren't out there." What is often true is that the recruiting sources used (word of mouth, traditional recruiters and advertisers, friend-of-a-friend, and other such means) do not reach or appeal to anyone but traditional candidates. The outcome is that only traditional candidates apply.

Another practice that occurs when trying to hire non-traditional candidates is that the interview process screens people out based on old methods of interviewing and making decisions. "Gut feel" and assumptions about how well the person will "fit in" are often the overriding issues. In a homogeneous workplace, it may be that finding someone who is different takes more effort. Leading this person may require different management practices and stronger interpersonal skills from co-workers. These underlying issues, rather than the applicant's job competence, can dominate the selection decision.

To ensure that they are interviewing and evaluating the person based on competence, managers can use a method called **behavioral interviewing.** In behavioral interviewing, the focus is on what the person has done in the past—the person's *actions,* not on what the person *says* he or she would *like* to do. Because of this, hypothetical "what-if" questions are not the primary factor, nor is the person's skill at being interviewed.

Retention

Once a person has been selected, the leader's primary task becomes effective development of the person's performance, which leads to satisfaction (and retention) on both the part of the employee and the organization. Dr. Susan Resnick-West, co-author of *Designing Performance Appraisal Systems,* discovered in working with numerous organizations that "the only predictor of the success of a performance management system is whether it is customized for individuals." This is another application of the Platinum Rule.

Clarity of expectations is important with all employees, and may be even more important with non-traditional employees, if they don't have easy access to the traditional information network. Once the person's performance expectations have been agreed on, he or she needs *meaningful feedback*—both positive and negative. Contrary to popular belief, *people want feedback*–even if it is not 100 percent positive. Most people would prefer knowing that they need to improve on a few things than not to know. Some leaders shy away from saying anything negative or from giving bad news, or they may think feedback will make no difference. In reality, not giving a "weaker" employee honest feedback deprives the person of the opportunity to improve. Then the negative self-fulfilling prophecy begins, and the employee is labeled as "not competent," without having the opportunity to improve. Providing appropriate *rewards and recognition* is the positive side of feedback. In leading a diverse workforce, the rewards and recognition need to be what the *employee* wants—not what the leader is most accustomed to giving. Leaders can simply ask people what they prefer for a job well done or can find innovative rewards from which the person can select (such as time off, being taken to lunch, a thank-you letter, and so forth).

Team Leadership

Leaders can begin to be inclusive within the team by observing the team on the following characteristics of group dynamics:

- Who talks and who listens? (Look for air time, interruptions, withdrawal from participating.)

- Who is influential? (Whose ideas are utilized and whose are not, who agrees or disagrees with whom?)

- How are decisions made? (By vote, consensus, compromise, mandate?)

- How is conflict managed? (Win-lose, avoidance, win-win?)

- How is feedback managed? (Encouraged, stifled?)

Then, after analyzing the answers to these questions, the leader can work with the group to establish positive rules, or norms, required for effective group interaction. The leader needs to give special attention to any elements of group dynamics that might be obstacles. Examples of positive group norms include:

- Open membership (All members, including new and non-traditional ones, are accepted with equal privileges.)

- Shared influence (on goals, decisions, priorities)

- Mutual respect

- Candor (People can challenge each other and disclose openly.)

Communication

Leaders also need to monitor their *own* communication processes with members of the team. The leader has an especially important role to play in communication and can demonstrate that he or she values all members by sharing information equally with everyone.

Informal social or communication networks exclude people from important opportunities to gain information. This structural issue is often a major obstacle to true inclusion. The people in the traditional network don't perceive any advantage associated with the network. However, if they think about information they have gained or relationships they have built as a result of their associations within these networks, or if they are asked to give these networks up, they often realize how important they have been (for example, the "golf group," after-hours gatherings, and so forth).

Other methods of informally sharing information can also exclude people. Because we tend to gravitate to people who are like us, we want to spend more time having lunch, doing projects, or even just chatting informally with them. Managers are in a position of special power and authority, and as such must share information with *everyone* who needs it, not just those with whom they are most comfortable.

Derailment Case Study

SIX MONTHS AGO, you took a big step in filling a job with a non-traditional employee. Previously, only traditional employees have held this job. It was a tough decision, and some people criticized you for it. Explaining to other traditional employees why they didn't get the job was tough, too. But you took the risk because Employee X had the skills, abilities, and experience needed to do the job. You were proud of your effort to go beyond the old stereotype of the job, and you felt good about Employee X's chances for success.

Now, six months later, things seem to be going wrong. Employee X seems to be struggling. The person doesn't know things a person in that position should know by now. Things seem to be taking too long to get done. On top of this, Employee X's peers are complaining, "We *knew* Employee X wouldn't work out." "This person just can't cut it here." "Why not send Employee X to department Y? That type does a lot better over there."

Employee X has come to you as well. "Why wasn't I invited to the planning meeting." Well, you thought it was too soon–you didn't want to overwhelm Employee X. "Why didn't I get a copy of the CEO's memo?" You just forgot–a natural mistake. "I feel like I don't know what I'm supposed to be doing." You *gave* Employee X a copy of the annual plan–why can't the person figure it out? You *did* notice a strange expression on Employee X's face when the gang was talking about the big outing last week. Why wasn't Employee X there?

You aren't sure why, but it's obvious that Employee X is becoming derailed.

Questions

What happened? What mistakes were made?

What aspects of structural inequality may have contributed to the situation?

As the manager, what would you do?

Diversity Mosaic Workshop Reaction Sheet for Leading Diversity

---

RATE YOUR LEVEL of agreement or disagreement with the following statements. Please answer candidly and write your general comments at the bottom. Your responses will remain anonymous and will help us to improve the workshop for future participants.

		Disagree		Neutral		Agree
1.	The concepts will help us to better respond to diversity trends.	1	2	3	4	5
2.	Written materials were informative and well-written.	1	2	3	4	5
3.	The audiovisual materials helped clarify the subject.	1	2	3	4	5
4.	The facilitator established an environment in which people felt free to openly share their views.	1	2	3	4	5
5.	The facilitator understood the subject and workshop content.	1	2	3	4	5
6.	The facilitator encouraged people to participate.	1	2	3	4	5
7.	I felt involved in the workshop.	1	2	3	4	5
8.	The facilitator helped me to relate ideas to my own experience.	1	2	3	4	5
9.	I understood the purpose of activities and how to complete them.	1	2	3	4	5
10.	The pace of the workshop was productive.	1	2	3	4	5

		Disagree	**Neutral**		**Agree**

11. I was enthusiastic about the workshop prior to attending.   1   2   3   4   5

12. My manager is a positive role model of valuing diversity.   1   2   3   4   5

13. I believe that this organization is committed to diversity and inclusion.   1   2   3   4   5

14. I am going to put into action what I learned in this session.   1   2   3   4   5

15. The most valuable part was _____

16. The least valuable part was _____

17. Comments (use extra paper if needed): _____

_____

_____

_____

_____

_____

_____

_____

_____

_____

_____

_____

_____

_____

_____

_____

_____

Leading Diversity: 360-Degree Assessment Instructions for Participants

FOLLOWING IS the information you need to complete the Leading Diversity 360-Degree Assessment, which has been designed to help you identify your strengths in the area of leading diversity and your developmental needs as part of your organization's diversity initiative. This feedback will act as a "mirror" to help you see yourself through the eyes of others who experience your behavior on a regular basis. While this type of assessment can feel a bit intimidating, it also provides you with a rare opportunity. Having this information gives you a "snapshot" you wouldn't normally have so that you can step back, reflect on the feedback, and take action to build on your strengths and make any desired improvements.

How It Works

As this feedback is "360 degree," it is designed to give you a look at yourself from above, below, and on the sides—all around. Try to select a variety of people as observers, people who see you in different situations. Select five to eight people who meet the following criteria:

- Regular, ongoing contact with you

- Have known you for at least six months

- Will give honest feedback (that is, won't just tell you what you want to hear, or have "an axe to grind")

- A combination of supportive people and challenging people

- Can complete the form and return it to the person doing the tabulating by the date given in the cover letter

For variety, you can select:

- Your boss

- People who report to you

- Your peers

- Your internal/external customers

(Please do NOT select family members or people outside your work environment.)

Note: You will need a minimum of five people to send in responses; fewer than that and the results will not be valid.

Complete the following steps:

1. Complete the Leading Diversity Self-Assessment Form on yourself, being sure to fill in your name. Immediately fax or send this to the person completing the tabulation.

2. Fill in your name, the due date, and the name of the person doing the tabulating on all five to eight of the Instructions for Observers cover letters you will use.

3. Give each of your observers a filled-in Instructions for Observers cover letter and a blank copy of the Leading Diversity: Assessment Form for Observers, both of which are contained in this workbook. All responses are anonymous, so do not put your observers' names on anything—only your own name for identification.

4. When they have finished, your observers should immediately fax or mail the completed assessment by the due date on the cover letter. Observers do not need to send or fax the instruction letter—only the form.

5. Assessments received after the due date cannot be included in your results, so make sure people complete them in time. If they cannot send a fax, make sure they mail their forms at least a week ahead of time.

The person doing the tabulating will compile the feedback and send you the results. No one will know your results but you and the person tabulating the results. Once you have the results, you can create your own personalized Developmental Action Plan.

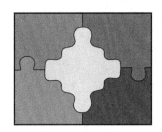

Leading Diversity:
Self-Assessment Form

Leading Diversity *Self-assessment Form*

Your name _____

Rate yourself openly and honestly on a scale of 1 to 5 for each item.

Role Modeling	Rarely		Sometimes		Often
1. I am a role model of valuing diversity to others.	1	2	3	4	5
2. I can communicate the value of diversity to others.	1	2	3	4	5
3. I have a strategy for learning about the differences, contributions, needs and priorities of each person who reports to me.	1	2	3	4	5
4. I acknowledge that people of different backgrounds can take different but equally effective approaches to their work, and I avoid turning those differences into stereotypes.	1	2	3	4	5
5. I do all I can to create a work environment in which all employees, customers, and community members are respected and valued.	1	2	3	4	5
6. I stretch beyond my comfort zone in reaching out to learn about and accept others who are different from me on dimensions with which I am uncomfortable.	1	2	3	4	5
Creating Structural Equality					
7. I understand employment and other laws and act to prevent instances of discrimination, harassment, and unequal opportunity.	1	2	3	4	5
8. I make an effort to recruit, select and promote nontraditional candidates.	1	2	3	4	5
9. I disregard physical characteristics when interviewing or selecting.	1	2	3	4	5
10. I consider people who are different from me for all opportunities, placements and promotions I have influence over.	1	2	3	4	5
11. I recognize and address biased or inappropriate words, humor, gestures and behaviors in others and in our organizational communications.	1	2	3	4	5
12. I ensure that expectations of people are clear.	1	2	3	4	5
13. I know how to create a motivating environment for a variety of people, both individually and as a group.	1	2	3	4	5
14. I take the biases of my own background into account when reviewing people's performance.	1	2	3	4	5
15. I give others honest feedback (both positive and negative) on their performance in a manner appropriate to each individual's needs.	1	2	3	4	5
16. I turn over responsibility to people who are different from me as often as I do to people who are like me.	1	2	3	4	5
17. I share unwritten rules with people who are different from me.	1	2	3	4	5
18. I keep all people equally in the information and informal networking loop.	1	2	3	4	5
19. I can fairly mediate conflicts when one person is similar to me and one is different.	1	2	3	4	5
20. I foresee situations with potential problems involving differences, and I take steps to prevent or defuse them.	1	2	3	4	5
21. I review our team's/organization's mission, strategies and goals to ensure that a diversity of views are included.	1	2	3	4	5
22. I actively look for instances of structural inequality, and take steps to correct them even if the issues are complex.	1	2	3	4	5

By: _____ **(due date) fax or send to:** _____.

Leading Diversity: Understanding and Using Your Assessment Results

ONCE THE PERSON tabulating the results completes your 360-degree Leading Diversity Assessment summary, he or she will send the results to you with certain information highlighted. The summary will include:

- All responses/scores summarized

- What others saw as your top three strongest areas

- What others saw as your three greatest areas for development

- Any questions on which the difference between your self-assessment and the summary was greater than 1 point (that is, areas in which you see yourself as stronger than others see you, or areas in which others see you as stronger than you saw yourself, which you may not feel as confident about)

- Any specific items of note or comments on the forms that were returned

Use the information as a tool for reflection, much like a "mirror" that shows how others perceive your ability to lead diversity at this point in time. However tempting it may be, please avoid trying to figure out who rated you on what. It's pure speculation and is beside the point.

The feedback is a tool to help you create your own Developmental Action Plan, found later in this workbook. To do this, pick one or two developmental areas and create personal goals for yourself. What you learned or will learn in the Diversity Mosaic: *Leading Diversity* workshop can help you with this. It can be helpful to share your goals with others within the organization, including those who gave you the feedback, to demonstrate to them that "we're all working on this together" and that you're going to take action based on the feedback. This is a great way to model your personal commitment to continually increasing your own level of diversity maturity, encouraging others to do the same.

It can also be helpful to work with other members of your team who attended, or will attend the workshop, to determine how you complement each other. Rather than sharing all your data, if you are not comfortable with that, just share your strongest areas and development areas to determine your team strengths as well as how you can support each other. You can also work together as peer coaches by agreeing to give each other ongoing feedback on how you're progressing toward your individual cultural competence goals.

You can also call the person designated as your organization's Diversity Change Agent if you would like to discuss the results or if you would like further assistance.

Leading Diversity: Developmental Action Plan

USE THIS FORM to summarize your results from the Leading Diversity Assessment and to create a personalized developmental plan that focuses on one or two goals for improvement based on the feedback you received.

Name: _____ Date: _____

Key Strengths I Can Build On

1. _____
2. _____
3. _____

Key Areas I Want to Develop

1. _____
2. _____
3. _____

Developmental Goals

Leading Diversity Goal 1: _____

Steps Required: _____

_____

Target Date for Accomplishment: _____

Benefits of Accomplishment: _____

Leading Diversity Goal 2: _____

Steps Required: _____

_____

Resources/People: _____

Target Date for Accomplishment: _____

Benefits of Accomplishment: _____

Notes: _____

_____

_____

Leading Diversity: 360–Degree Assessment Instructions for Observers

---

HELLO!

As part of our organization's diversity initiative, _____ [participant's name] is asking for feedback on his/her skills in leading diversity. Because you work closely with this person, he/she has selected you to give some feedback that will help him/her identify strengths to build on and areas to develop. In effect, you will be a "mirror" that will help the person see him- or herself more clearly. The person will use your feedback, combined with the feedback of others, to develop a personalized action plan to develop additional ability to lead diversity. This will help him/her to effectively champion your organization's diversity initiative as a leader.

All responses will remain anonymous. The person you're rating will not see the form you fill out. It will go straight to the person tabulating the results, who will compile your ratings with the ratings from four to eight other people. These will go into a synthesized report that will be given to the person being assessed.

Please answer the questions candidly, based on the person's actions that you have observed. Please do not just tell him or her what you think he or she wants to hear. If you slant your feedback, the person won't have the chance to see him- or herself in an accurate mirror. Please DO NOT put your name on this form. Only write the name *of the person you're rating* on the form (if it hasn't been filled in already).

Here are the steps:

1. When you have finished, send the form to the person tabulating the results by _____ [due date]. Do not send this instruction letter—just the form.

2. Forms received after the due date cannot be included in the results, so make sure you complete it in time. If you cannot hand deliver it or send a fax, make sure you mail it at least a week ahead of time.

3. Fax or send to: _____
    [name of person tabulating results]. Fax number, phone number, and mailing address:

    _____

    _____

Use the following as a reference when completing the assessment:

*   **Cultural Competence** is defined as "A set of competencies and skills that individuals and organizations use to create a truly inclusive environment that values diversity."
*   **Diversity** is defined as "The mosaic of people who bring a variety of backgrounds, styles, perspectives, beliefs, and competencies as assets to the groups and individuals with whom they interact." Examples of **dimensions of diversity** include age, race, ethnic heritage, mental/physical abilities, gender, sexual orientation, education, religion, marital and parental status, work background, income, geographic location, personality style, and so on.
*   **Non-traditional employee** is defined as "employees whose dimensions of diversity are different from those of the people traditionally employed in that job."

Thank you for your valued input!

Leading Diversity: 360–Degree Assessment Instructions for Observers

---

HELLO!

As part of our organization's diversity initiative, _____ [participant's name] is asking for feedback on his/her skills in leading diversity. Because you work closely with this person, he/she has selected you to give some feedback that will help him/her identify strengths to build on and areas to develop. In effect, you will be a "mirror" that will help the person see him- or herself more clearly. The person will use your feedback, combined with the feedback of others, to develop a personalized action plan to develop additional ability to lead diversity. This will help him/her to effectively champion your organization's diversity initiative as a leader.

All responses will remain anonymous. The person you're rating will not see the form you fill out. It will go straight to the person tabulating the results, who will compile your ratings with the ratings from four to eight other people. These will go into a synthesized report that will be given to the person being assessed.

Please answer the questions candidly, based on the person's actions that you have observed. Please do not just tell him or her what you think he or she wants to hear. If you slant your feedback, the person won't have the chance to see him- or herself in an accurate mirror. Please DO NOT put your name on this form. Only write the name *of the person you're rating* on the form (if it hasn't been filled in already).

Here are the steps:

1. When you have finished, send the form to the person tabulating the results by _____ [due date]. Do not send this instruction letter—just the form.

2. Forms received after the due date cannot be included in the results, so make sure you complete it in time. If you cannot hand deliver it or send a fax, make sure you mail it at least a week ahead of time.

3. Fax or send to: _____
    [name of person tabulating results]. Fax number, phone number, and mailing address:

    _____

    _____

Use the following as a reference when completing the assessment:

*   **Cultural Competence** is defined as "A set of competencies and skills that individuals and organizations use to create a truly inclusive environment that values diversity."
*   **Diversity** is defined as "The mosaic of people who bring a variety of backgrounds, styles, perspectives, beliefs, and competencies as assets to the groups and individuals with whom they interact." Examples of **dimensions of diversity** include age, race, ethnic heritage, mental/physical abilities, gender, sexual orientation, education, religion, marital and parental status, work background, income, geographic location, personality style, and so on.
*   **Non-traditional employee** is defined as "employees whose dimensions of diversity are different from those of the people traditionally employed in that job."

Thank you for your valued input!

Leading Diversity: 360–Degree Assessment Instructions for Observers

HELLO!

As part of our organization's diversity initiative, _____ [participant's name] is asking for feedback on his/her skills in leading diversity. Because you work closely with this person, he/she has selected you to give some feedback that will help him/her identify strengths to build on and areas to develop. In effect, you will be a "mirror" that will help the person see him- or herself more clearly. The person will use your feedback, combined with the feedback of others, to develop a personalized action plan to develop additional ability to lead diversity. This will help him/her to effectively champion your organization's diversity initiative as a leader.

All responses will remain anonymous. The person you're rating will not see the form you fill out. It will go straight to the person tabulating the results, who will compile your ratings with the ratings from four to eight other people. These will go into a synthesized report that will be given to the person being assessed.

Please answer the questions candidly, based on the person's actions that you have observed. Please do not just tell him or her what you think he or she wants to hear. If you slant your feedback, the person won't have the chance to see him- or herself in an accurate mirror. Please DO NOT put your name on this form. Only write the name *of the person you're rating* on the form (if it hasn't been filled in already).

Here are the steps:

1. When you have finished, send the form to the person tabulating the results by _____ [due date]. Do not send this instruction letter—just the form.

2. Forms received after the due date cannot be included in the results, so make sure you complete it in time. If you cannot hand deliver it or send a fax, make sure you mail it at least a week ahead of time.

3. Fax or send to: _____
    [name of person tabulating results]. Fax number, phone number, and mailing address:

    _____

    _____

Use the following as a reference when completing the assessment:

*   **Cultural Competence** is defined as "A set of competencies and skills that individuals and organizations use to create a truly inclusive environment that values diversity."
*   **Diversity** is defined as "The mosaic of people who bring a variety of backgrounds, styles, perspectives, beliefs, and competencies as assets to the groups and individuals with whom they interact." Examples of **dimensions of diversity** include age, race, ethnic heritage, mental/physical abilities, gender, sexual orientation, education, religion, marital and parental status, work background, income, geographic location, personality style, and so on.
*   **Non-traditional employee** is defined as "employees whose dimensions of diversity are different from those of the people traditionally employed in that job."

Thank you for your valued input!

Leading Diversity: 360-Degree Assessment Instructions for Observers

HELLO!

As part of our organization's diversity initiative, _____ [participant's name] is asking for feedback on his/her skills in leading diversity. Because you work closely with this person, he/she has selected you to give some feedback that will help him/her identify strengths to build on and areas to develop. In effect, you will be a "mirror" that will help the person see him- or herself more clearly. The person will use your feedback, combined with the feedback of others, to develop a personalized action plan to develop additional ability to lead diversity. This will help him/her to effectively champion your organization's diversity initiative as a leader.

All responses will remain anonymous. The person you're rating will not see the form you fill out. It will go straight to the person tabulating the results, who will compile your ratings with the ratings from four to eight other people. These will go into a synthesized report that will be given to the person being assessed.

Please answer the questions candidly, based on the person's actions that you have observed. Please do not just tell him or her what you think he or she wants to hear. If you slant your feedback, the person won't have the chance to see him- or herself in an accurate mirror. Please DO NOT put your name on this form. Only write the name *of the person you're rating* on the form (if it hasn't been filled in already).

Here are the steps:

1. When you have finished, send the form to the person tabulating the results by _____ [due date]. Do not send this instruction letter—just the form.

2. Forms received after the due date cannot be included in the results, so make sure you complete it in time. If you cannot hand deliver it or send a fax, make sure you mail it at least a week ahead of time.

3. Fax or send to: _____
    [name of person tabulating results]. Fax number, phone number, and mailing address:

    _____

    _____

Use the following as a reference when completing the assessment:

*   **Cultural Competence** is defined as "A set of competencies and skills that individuals and organizations use to create a truly inclusive environment that values diversity."
*   **Diversity** is defined as "The mosaic of people who bring a variety of backgrounds, styles, perspectives, beliefs, and competencies as assets to the groups and individuals with whom they interact." Examples of **dimensions of diversity** include age, race, ethnic heritage, mental/physical abilities, gender, sexual orientation, education, religion, marital and parental status, work background, income, geographic location, personality style, and so on.
*   **Non-traditional employee** is defined as "employees whose dimensions of diversity are different from those of the people traditionally employed in that job."

Thank you for your valued input!

Leading Diversity: 360–Degree Assessment Instructions for Observers

HELLO!

As part of our organization's diversity initiative, _____ [participant's name] is asking for feedback on his/her skills in leading diversity. Because you work closely with this person, he/she has selected you to give some feedback that will help him/her identify strengths to build on and areas to develop. In effect, you will be a "mirror" that will help the person see him- or herself more clearly. The person will use your feedback, combined with the feedback of others, to develop a personalized action plan to develop additional ability to lead diversity. This will help him/her to effectively champion your organization's diversity initiative as a leader.

All responses will remain anonymous. The person you're rating will not see the form you fill out. It will go straight to the person tabulating the results, who will compile your ratings with the ratings from four to eight other people. These will go into a synthesized report that will be given to the person being assessed.

Please answer the questions candidly, based on the person's actions that you have observed. Please do not just tell him or her what you think he or she wants to hear. If you slant your feedback, the person won't have the chance to see him- or herself in an accurate mirror. Please DO NOT put your name on this form. Only write the name *of the person you're rating* on the form (if it hasn't been filled in already).

Here are the steps:

1. When you have finished, send the form to the person tabulating the results by _____ [due date]. Do not send this instruction letter—just the form.

2. Forms received after the due date cannot be included in the results, so make sure you complete it in time. If you cannot hand deliver it or send a fax, make sure you mail it at least a week ahead of time.

3. Fax or send to: _____
   [name of person tabulating results]. Fax number, phone number, and mailing address:

   _____

   _____

Use the following as a reference when completing the assessment:

- **Cultural Competence** is defined as "A set of competencies and skills that individuals and organizations use to create a truly inclusive environment that values diversity."
- **Diversity** is defined as "The mosaic of people who bring a variety of backgrounds, styles, perspectives, beliefs, and competencies as assets to the groups and individuals with whom they interact." Examples of **dimensions of diversity** include age, race, ethnic heritage, mental/physical abilities, gender, sexual orientation, education, religion, marital and parental status, work background, income, geographic location, personality style, and so on.
- **Non-traditional employee** is defined as "employees whose dimensions of diversity are different from those of the people traditionally employed in that job."

Thank you for your valued input!

Leading Diversity: 360–Degree Assessment Instructions for Observers

---

HELLO!

As part of our organization's diversity initiative, _____ [participant's name] is asking for feedback on his/her skills in leading diversity. Because you work closely with this person, he/she has selected you to give some feedback that will help him/her identify strengths to build on and areas to develop. In effect, you will be a "mirror" that will help the person see him- or herself more clearly. The person will use your feedback, combined with the feedback of others, to develop a personalized action plan to develop additional ability to lead diversity. This will help him/her to effectively champion your organization's diversity initiative as a leader.

All responses will remain anonymous. The person you're rating will not see the form you fill out. It will go straight to the person tabulating the results, who will compile your ratings with the ratings from four to eight other people. These will go into a synthesized report that will be given to the person being assessed.

Please answer the questions candidly, based on the person's actions that you have observed. Please do not just tell him or her what you think he or she wants to hear. If you slant your feedback, the person won't have the chance to see him- or herself in an accurate mirror. Please DO NOT put your name on this form. Only write the name *of the person you're rating* on the form (if it hasn't been filled in already).

Here are the steps:

1. When you have finished, send the form to the person tabulating the results by _____ [due date]. Do not send this instruction letter—just the form.

2. Forms received after the due date cannot be included in the results, so make sure you complete it in time. If you cannot hand deliver it or send a fax, make sure you mail it at least a week ahead of time.

3. Fax or send to: _____
    [name of person tabulating results]. Fax number, phone number, and mailing address:

    _____

    _____

Use the following as a reference when completing the assessment:

*   **Cultural Competence** is defined as "A set of competencies and skills that individuals and organizations use to create a truly inclusive environment that values diversity."
*   **Diversity** is defined as "The mosaic of people who bring a variety of backgrounds, styles, perspectives, beliefs, and competencies as assets to the groups and individuals with whom they interact." Examples of **dimensions of diversity** include age, race, ethnic heritage, mental/physical abilities, gender, sexual orientation, education, religion, marital and parental status, work background, income, geographic location, personality style, and so on.
*   **Non-traditional employee** is defined as "employees whose dimensions of diversity are different from those of the people traditionally employed in that job."

Thank you for your valued input!

Leading Diversity: 360-Degree Assessment Instructions for Observers

HELLO!

As part of our organization's diversity initiative, _____ [participant's name] is asking for feedback on his/her skills in leading diversity. Because you work closely with this person, he/she has selected you to give some feedback that will help him/her identify strengths to build on and areas to develop. In effect, you will be a "mirror" that will help the person see him- or herself more clearly. The person will use your feedback, combined with the feedback of others, to develop a personalized action plan to develop additional ability to lead diversity. This will help him/her to effectively champion your organization's diversity initiative as a leader.

All responses will remain anonymous. The person you're rating will not see the form you fill out. It will go straight to the person tabulating the results, who will compile your ratings with the ratings from four to eight other people. These will go into a synthesized report that will be given to the person being assessed.

Please answer the questions candidly, based on the person's actions that you have observed. Please do not just tell him or her what you think he or she wants to hear. If you slant your feedback, the person won't have the chance to see him- or herself in an accurate mirror. Please DO NOT put your name on this form. Only write the name *of the person you're rating* on the form (if it hasn't been filled in already).

Here are the steps:

1. When you have finished, send the form to the person tabulating the results by _____ [due date]. Do not send this instruction letter—just the form.

2. Forms received after the due date cannot be included in the results, so make sure you complete it in time. If you cannot hand deliver it or send a fax, make sure you mail it at least a week ahead of time.

3. Fax or send to: _____
    [name of person tabulating results]. Fax number, phone number, and mailing address:

    _____

    _____

Use the following as a reference when completing the assessment:

-   **Cultural Competence** is defined as "A set of competencies and skills that individuals and organizations use to create a truly inclusive environment that values diversity."
-   **Diversity** is defined as "The mosaic of people who bring a variety of backgrounds, styles, perspectives, beliefs, and competencies as assets to the groups and individuals with whom they interact." Examples of **dimensions of diversity** include age, race, ethnic heritage, mental/physical abilities, gender, sexual orientation, education, religion, marital and parental status, work background, income, geographic location, personality style, and so on.
-   **Non-traditional employee** is defined as "employees whose dimensions of diversity are different from those of the people traditionally employed in that job."

Thank you for your valued input!

Leading Diversity: 360-Degree Assessment Instructions for Observers

---

HELLO!

As part of our organization's diversity initiative, _____ [participant's name] is asking for feedback on his/her skills in leading diversity. Because you work closely with this person, he/she has selected you to give some feedback that will help him/her identify strengths to build on and areas to develop. In effect, you will be a "mirror" that will help the person see him- or herself more clearly. The person will use your feedback, combined with the feedback of others, to develop a personalized action plan to develop additional ability to lead diversity. This will help him/her to effectively champion your organization's diversity initiative as a leader.

All responses will remain anonymous. The person you're rating will not see the form you fill out. It will go straight to the person tabulating the results, who will compile your ratings with the ratings from four to eight other people. These will go into a synthesized report that will be given to the person being assessed.

Please answer the questions candidly, based on the person's actions that you have observed. Please do not just tell him or her what you think he or she wants to hear. If you slant your feedback, the person won't have the chance to see him- or herself in an accurate mirror. Please DO NOT put your name on this form. Only write the name *of the person you're rating* on the form (if it hasn't been filled in already).

Here are the steps:

1. When you have finished, send the form to the person tabulating the results by _____ [due date]. Do not send this instruction letter—just the form.

2. Forms received after the due date cannot be included in the results, so make sure you complete it in time. If you cannot hand deliver it or send a fax, make sure you mail it at least a week ahead of time.

3. Fax or send to: _____
   [name of person tabulating results]. Fax number, phone number, and mailing address:

   _____

   _____

Use the following as a reference when completing the assessment:

- **Cultural Competence** is defined as "A set of competencies and skills that individuals and organizations use to create a truly inclusive environment that values diversity."
- **Diversity** is defined as "The mosaic of people who bring a variety of backgrounds, styles, perspectives, beliefs, and competencies as assets to the groups and individuals with whom they interact." Examples of **dimensions of diversity** include age, race, ethnic heritage, mental/physical abilities, gender, sexual orientation, education, religion, marital and parental status, work background, income, geographic location, personality style, and so on.
- **Non-traditional employee** is defined as "employees whose dimensions of diversity are different from those of the people traditionally employed in that job."

Thank you for your valued input!

Leading Diversity: Assessment Form for Observers

Name of the person being observed _____
Rate the person openly and honestly on a scale of 1 to 5 for each item.

Role Modeling—The person:	Rarely		Sometimes		Often
1. Is a role model of valuing diversity to others.	1	2	3	4	5
2. Can communicate the value of diversity to others.	1	2	3	4	5
3. Has a strategy for learning about the differences, contributions, needs and priorities of each person who reports to him/her.	1	2	3	4	5
4. Acknowledges that people of different backgrounds can take different but equally effective approaches to their work, and avoids turning those differences into stereotypes.	1	2	3	4	5
5. Does all he/she can to create a work environment in which all employees, customers, and community members are respected and valued.	1	2	3	4	5
6. Stretches beyond his/her comfort zone in reaching out to learn about and accept others who are different from him/her on dimensions with which he/she is uncomfortable.	1	2	3	4	5
Creating Structural Equality—The person:					
7. Understands employment and other laws and acts to prevent instances of discrimination, harassment, and unequal opportunity.	1	2	3	4	5
8. Makes an effort to recruit, select and promote nontraditional candidates.	1	2	3	4	5
9. Disregards physical characteristics when interviewing/selecting.	1	2	3	4	5
10. Considers people who are different from him/her for all opportunities, placements and promotions he/she has influence over.	1	2	3	4	5
11. Recognizes and addresses biased or inappropriate words, humor, gestures and behaviors in others and in our organizational communications.	1	2	3	4	5
12. Ensures that expectations of people are clear.	1	2	3	4	5
13. Creates a motivating environment for a variety of people, both individually and as a group.	1	2	3	4	5
14. Takes the biases of his/her own background into account when reviewing people's performance.	1	2	3	4	5
15. Gives others honest feedback (both positive and negative) on their performance in a manner appropriate to each individual's needs.	1	2	3	4	5
16. Turns over responsibility to people who are different from him/her as often as he/she does to people who are like him/her.	1	2	3	4	5
17. Shares unwritten rules with people who are different from him/her.	1	2	3	4	5
18. Keeps all people equally in the information and informal networking loop.	1	2	3	4	5
19. Fairly mediates conflicts when one person is similar to him/her and one is different.	1	2	3	4	5
20. Foresees situations with potential problems involving differences, and takes steps to prevent or defuse them.	1	2	3	4	5
21. Review the team's/organization's mission, strategies and goals to ensure that a diversity of views are included.	1	2	3	4	5
22. Actively looks for instances of structural inequality, and takes steps to correct them even if the issues are complex.	1	2	3	4	5

By: _____ **(due date) fax or send to:** _____.

You do not need to send the instruction letter, just this form.

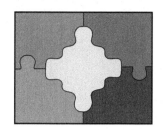

Leading Diversity: Assessment Form for Observers

Name of the person being observed _____
Rate the person openly and honestly on a scale of 1 to 5 for each item.

Role Modeling—The person:	Rarely		Sometimes		Often
1. Is a role model of valuing diversity to others.	1	2	3	4	5
2. Can communicate the value of diversity to others.	1	2	3	4	5
3. Has a strategy for learning about the differences, contributions, needs and priorities of each person who reports to him/her.	1	2	3	4	5
4. Acknowledges that people of different backgrounds can take different but equally effective approaches to their work, and avoids turning those differences into stereotypes.	1	2	3	4	5
5. Does all he/she can to create a work environment in which all employees, customers, and community members are respected and valued.	1	2	3	4	5
6. Stretches beyond his/her comfort zone in reaching out to learn about and accept others who are different from him/her on dimensions with which he/she is uncomfortable.	1	2	3	4	5
Creating Structural Equality—The person:					
7. Understands employment and other laws and acts to prevent instances of discrimination, harassment, and unequal opportunity.	1	2	3	4	5
8. Makes an effort to recruit, select and promote nontraditional candidates.	1	2	3	4	5
9. Disregards physical characteristics when interviewing/selecting.	1	2	3	4	5
10. Considers people who are different from him/her for all opportunities, placements and promotions he/she has influence over.	1	2	3	4	5
11. Recognizes and addresses biased or inappropriate words, humor, gestures and behaviors in others and in our organizational communications.	1	2	3	4	5
12. Ensures that expectations of people are clear.	1	2	3	4	5
13. Creates a motivating environment for a variety of people, both individually and as a group.	1	2	3	4	5
14. Takes the biases of his/her own background into account when reviewing people's performance.	1	2	3	4	5
15. Gives others honest feedback (both positive and negative) on their performance in a manner appropriate to each individual's needs.	1	2	3	4	5
16. Turns over responsibility to people who are different from him/her as often as he/she does to people who are like him/her.	1	2	3	4	5
17. Shares unwritten rules with people who are different from him/her.	1	2	3	4	5
18. Keeps all people equally in the information and informal networking loop.	1	2	3	4	5
19. Fairly mediates conflicts when one person is similar to him/her and one is different.	1	2	3	4	5
20. Foresees situations with potential problems involving differences, and takes steps to prevent or defuse them.	1	2	3	4	5
21. Review the team's/organization's mission, strategies and goals to ensure that a diversity of views are included.	1	2	3	4	5
22. Actively looks for instances of structural inequality, and takes steps to correct them even if the issues are complex.	1	2	3	4	5

By: _____ **(due date) fax or send to:** _____.

You do not need to send the instruction letter, just this form.

Leading Diversity: Assessment Form for Observers

Name of the person being observed _____
Rate the person openly and honestly on a scale of 1 to 5 for each item.

Role Modeling—The person:	Rarely		Sometimes		Often
1. Is a role model of valuing diversity to others.	1	2	3	4	5
2. Can communicate the value of diversity to others.	1	2	3	4	5
3. Has a strategy for learning about the differences, contributions, needs and priorities of each person who reports to him/her.	1	2	3	4	5
4. Acknowledges that people of different backgrounds can take different but equally effective approaches to their work, and avoids turning those differences into stereotypes.	1	2	3	4	5
5. Does all he/she can to create a work environment in which all employees, customers, and community members are respected and valued.	1	2	3	4	5
6. Stretches beyond his/her comfort zone in reaching out to learn about and accept others who are different from him/her on dimensions with which he/she is uncomfortable.	1	2	3	4	5
Creating Structural Equality—The person:					
7. Understands employment and other laws and acts to prevent instances of discrimination, harassment, and unequal opportunity.	1	2	3	4	5
8. Makes an effort to recruit, select and promote nontraditional candidates.	1	2	3	4	5
9. Disregards physical characteristics when interviewing/selecting.	1	2	3	4	5
10. Considers people who are different from him/her for all opportunities, placements and promotions he/she has influence over.	1	2	3	4	5
11. Recognizes and addresses biased or inappropriate words, humor, gestures and behaviors in others and in our organizational communications.	1	2	3	4	5
12. Ensures that expectations of people are clear.	1	2	3	4	5
13. Creates a motivating environment for a variety of people, both individually and as a group.	1	2	3	4	5
14. Takes the biases of his/her own background into account when reviewing people's performance.	1	2	3	4	5
15. Gives others honest feedback (both positive and negative) on their performance in a manner appropriate to each individual's needs.	1	2	3	4	5
16. Turns over responsibility to people who are different from him/her as often as he/she does to people who are like him/her.	1	2	3	4	5
17. Shares unwritten rules with people who are different from him/her.	1	2	3	4	5
18. Keeps all people equally in the information and informal networking loop.	1	2	3	4	5
19. Fairly mediates conflicts when one person is similar to him/her and one is different.	1	2	3	4	5
20. Foresees situations with potential problems involving differences, and takes steps to prevent or defuse them.	1	2	3	4	5
21. Review the team's/organization's mission, strategies and goals to ensure that a diversity of views are included.	1	2	3	4	5
22. Actively looks for instances of structural inequality, and takes steps to correct them even if the issues are complex.	1	2	3	4	5

By: _____ **(due date) fax or send to:** _____.

You do not need to send the instruction letter, just this form.

Leading Diversity: Assessment Form for Observers

Name of the person being observed _____
Rate the person openly and honestly on a scale of 1 to 5 for each item.

Role Modeling—The person:	Rarely		Sometimes		Often
1. Is a role model of valuing diversity to others.	1	2	3	4	5
2. Can communicate the value of diversity to others.	1	2	3	4	5
3. Has a strategy for learning about the differences, contributions, needs and priorities of each person who reports to him/her.	1	2	3	4	5
4. Acknowledges that people of different backgrounds can take different but equally effective approaches to their work, and avoids turning those differences into stereotypes.	1	2	3	4	5
5. Does all he/she can to create a work environment in which all employees, customers, and community members are respected and valued.	1	2	3	4	5
6. Stretches beyond his/her comfort zone in reaching out to learn about and accept others who are different from him/her on dimensions with which he/she is uncomfortable.	1	2	3	4	5
Creating Structural Equality—The person:					
7. Understands employment and other laws and acts to prevent instances of discrimination, harassment, and unequal opportunity.	1	2	3	4	5
8. Makes an effort to recruit, select and promote nontraditional candidates.	1	2	3	4	5
9. Disregards physical characteristics when interviewing/selecting.	1	2	3	4	5
10. Considers people who are different from him/her for all opportunities, placements and promotions he/she has influence over.	1	2	3	4	5
11. Recognizes and addresses biased or inappropriate words, humor, gestures and behaviors in others and in our organizational communications.	1	2	3	4	5
12. Ensures that expectations of people are clear.	1	2	3	4	5
13. Creates a motivating environment for a variety of people, both individually and as a group.	1	2	3	4	5
14. Takes the biases of his/her own background into account when reviewing people's performance.	1	2	3	4	5
15. Gives others honest feedback (both positive and negative) on their performance in a manner appropriate to each individual's needs.	1	2	3	4	5
16. Turns over responsibility to people who are different from him/her as often as he/she does to people who are like him/her.	1	2	3	4	5
17. Shares unwritten rules with people who are different from him/her.	1	2	3	4	5
18. Keeps all people equally in the information and informal networking loop.	1	2	3	4	5
19. Fairly mediates conflicts when one person is similar to him/her and one is different.	1	2	3	4	5
20. Foresees situations with potential problems involving differences, and takes steps to prevent or defuse them.	1	2	3	4	5
21. Review the team's/organization's mission, strategies and goals to ensure that a diversity of views are included.	1	2	3	4	5
22. Actively looks for instances of structural inequality, and takes steps to correct them even if the issues are complex.	1	2	3	4	5

By: _____ **(due date) fax or send to:** _____.

You do not need to send the instruction letter, just this form.

Leading Diversity: Assessment Form for Observers

Name of the person being observed _____

Rate the person openly and honestly on a scale of 1 to 5 for each item.

Role Modeling—The person:	Rarely		Sometimes		Often
1. Is a role model of valuing diversity to others.	1	2	3	4	5
2. Can communicate the value of diversity to others.	1	2	3	4	5
3. Has a strategy for learning about the differences, contributions, needs and priorities of each person who reports to him/her.	1	2	3	4	5
4. Acknowledges that people of different backgrounds can take different but equally effective approaches to their work, and avoids turning those differences into stereotypes.	1	2	3	4	5
5. Does all he/she can to create a work environment in which all employees, customers, and community members are respected and valued.	1	2	3	4	5
6. Stretches beyond his/her comfort zone in reaching out to learn about and accept others who are different from him/her on dimensions with which he/she is uncomfortable.	1	2	3	4	5
Creating Structural Equality—The person:					
7. Understands employment and other laws and acts to prevent instances of discrimination, harassment, and unequal opportunity.	1	2	3	4	5
8. Makes an effort to recruit, select and promote nontraditional candidates.	1	2	3	4	5
9. Disregards physical characteristics when interviewing/selecting.	1	2	3	4	5
10. Considers people who are different from him/her for all opportunities, placements and promotions he/she has influence over.	1	2	3	4	5
11. Recognizes and addresses biased or inappropriate words, humor, gestures and behaviors in others and in our organizational communications.	1	2	3	4	5
12. Ensures that expectations of people are clear.	1	2	3	4	5
13. Creates a motivating environment for a variety of people, both individually and as a group.	1	2	3	4	5
14. Takes the biases of his/her own background into account when reviewing people's performance.	1	2	3	4	5
15. Gives others honest feedback (both positive and negative) on their performance in a manner appropriate to each individual's needs.	1	2	3	4	5
16. Turns over responsibility to people who are different from him/her as often as he/she does to people who are like him/her.	1	2	3	4	5
17. Shares unwritten rules with people who are different from him/her.	1	2	3	4	5
18. Keeps all people equally in the information and informal networking loop.	1	2	3	4	5
19. Fairly mediates conflicts when one person is similar to him/her and one is different.	1	2	3	4	5
20. Foresees situations with potential problems involving differences, and takes steps to prevent or defuse them.	1	2	3	4	5
21. Review the team's/organization's mission, strategies and goals to ensure that a diversity of views are included.	1	2	3	4	5
22. Actively looks for instances of structural inequality, and takes steps to correct them even if the issues are complex.	1	2	3	4	5

By: _____ **(due date) fax or send to:** _____.

You do not need to send the instruction letter, just this form.

Leading Diversity: Assessment Form for Observers

Name of the person being observed _____
Rate the person openly and honestly on a scale of 1 to 5 for each item.

Role Modeling—The person:	Rarely		Sometimes		Often
1. Is a role model of valuing diversity to others.	1	2	3	4	5
2. Can communicate the value of diversity to others.	1	2	3	4	5
3. Has a strategy for learning about the differences, contributions, needs and priorities of each person who reports to him/her.	1	2	3	4	5
4. Acknowledges that people of different backgrounds can take different but equally effective approaches to their work, and avoids turning those differences into stereotypes.	1	2	3	4	5
5. Does all he/she can to create a work environment in which all employees, customers, and community members are respected and valued.	1	2	3	4	5
6. Stretches beyond his/her comfort zone in reaching out to learn about and accept others who are different from him/her on dimensions with which he/she is uncomfortable.	1	2	3	4	5
Creating Structural Equality—The person:					
7. Understands employment and other laws and acts to prevent instances of discrimination, harassment, and unequal opportunity.	1	2	3	4	5
8. Makes an effort to recruit, select and promote nontraditional candidates.	1	2	3	4	5
9. Disregards physical characteristics when interviewing/selecting.	1	2	3	4	5
10. Considers people who are different from him/her for all opportunities, placements and promotions he/she has influence over.	1	2	3	4	5
11. Recognizes and addresses biased or inappropriate words, humor, gestures and behaviors in others and in our organizational communications.	1	2	3	4	5
12. Ensures that expectations of people are clear.	1	2	3	4	5
13. Creates a motivating environment for a variety of people, both individually and as a group.	1	2	3	4	5
14. Takes the biases of his/her own background into account when reviewing people's performance.	1	2	3	4	5
15. Gives others honest feedback (both positive and negative) on their performance in a manner appropriate to each individual's needs.	1	2	3	4	5
16. Turns over responsibility to people who are different from him/her as often as he/she does to people who are like him/her.	1	2	3	4	5
17. Shares unwritten rules with people who are different from him/her.	1	2	3	4	5
18. Keeps all people equally in the information and informal networking loop.	1	2	3	4	5
19. Fairly mediates conflicts when one person is similar to him/her and one is different.	1	2	3	4	5
20. Foresees situations with potential problems involving differences, and takes steps to prevent or defuse them.	1	2	3	4	5
21. Review the team's/organization's mission, strategies and goals to ensure that a diversity of views are included.	1	2	3	4	5
22. Actively looks for instances of structural inequality, and takes steps to correct them even if the issues are complex.	1	2	3	4	5

By: _____ **(due date) fax or send to:** _____.

You do not need to send the instruction letter, just this form.

Leading Diversity: Assessment Form for Observers

Name of the person being observed _____
Rate the person openly and honestly on a scale of 1 to 5 for each item.

Role Modeling—The person:	Rarely		Sometimes		Often
1. Is a role model of valuing diversity to others.	1	2	3	4	5
2. Can communicate the value of diversity to others.	1	2	3	4	5
3. Has a strategy for learning about the differences, contributions, needs and priorities of each person who reports to him/her.	1	2	3	4	5
4. Acknowledges that people of different backgrounds can take different but equally effective approaches to their work, and avoids turning those differences into stereotypes.	1	2	3	4	5
5. Does all he/she can to create a work environment in which all employees, customers, and community members are respected and valued.	1	2	3	4	5
6. Stretches beyond his/her comfort zone in reaching out to learn about and accept others who are different from him/her on dimensions with which he/she is uncomfortable.	1	2	3	4	5
Creating Structural Equality—The person:					
7. Understands employment and other laws and acts to prevent instances of discrimination, harassment, and unequal opportunity.	1	2	3	4	5
8. Makes an effort to recruit, select and promote nontraditional candidates.	1	2	3	4	5
9. Disregards physical characteristics when interviewing/selecting.	1	2	3	4	5
10. Considers people who are different from him/her for all opportunities, placements and promotions he/she has influence over.	1	2	3	4	5
11. Recognizes and addresses biased or inappropriate words, humor, gestures and behaviors in others and in our organizational communications.	1	2	3	4	5
12. Ensures that expectations of people are clear.	1	2	3	4	5
13. Creates a motivating environment for a variety of people, both individually and as a group.	1	2	3	4	5
14. Takes the biases of his/her own background into account when reviewing people's performance.	1	2	3	4	5
15. Gives others honest feedback (both positive and negative) on their performance in a manner appropriate to each individual's needs.	1	2	3	4	5
16. Turns over responsibility to people who are different from him/her as often as he/she does to people who are like him/her.	1	2	3	4	5
17. Shares unwritten rules with people who are different from him/her.	1	2	3	4	5
18. Keeps all people equally in the information and informal networking loop.	1	2	3	4	5
19. Fairly mediates conflicts when one person is similar to him/her and one is different.	1	2	3	4	5
20. Foresees situations with potential problems involving differences, and takes steps to prevent or defuse them.	1	2	3	4	5
21. Review the team's/organization's mission, strategies and goals to ensure that a diversity of views are included.	1	2	3	4	5
22. Actively looks for instances of structural inequality, and takes steps to correct them even if the issues are complex.	1	2	3	4	5

By: _____ **(due date) fax or send to:** _____.

You do not need to send the instruction letter, just this form.

Leading Diversity: Assessment Form for Observers

Name of the person being observed _____
Rate the person openly and honestly on a scale of 1 to 5 for each item.

Role Modeling—The person:	Rarely		Sometimes		Often
1. Is a role model of valuing diversity to others.	1	2	3	4	5
2. Can communicate the value of diversity to others.	1	2	3	4	5
3. Has a strategy for learning about the differences, contributions, needs and priorities of each person who reports to him/her.	1	2	3	4	5
4. Acknowledges that people of different backgrounds can take different but equally effective approaches to their work, and avoids turning those differences into stereotypes.	1	2	3	4	5
5. Does all he/she can to create a work environment in which all employees, customers, and community members are respected and valued.	1	2	3	4	5
6. Stretches beyond his/her comfort zone in reaching out to learn about and accept others who are different from him/her on dimensions with which he/she is uncomfortable.	1	2	3	4	5
Creating Structural Equality—The person:					
7. Understands employment and other laws and acts to prevent instances of discrimination, harassment, and unequal opportunity.	1	2	3	4	5
8. Makes an effort to recruit, select and promote nontraditional candidates.	1	2	3	4	5
9. Disregards physical characteristics when interviewing/selecting.	1	2	3	4	5
10. Considers people who are different from him/her for all opportunities, placements and promotions he/she has influence over.	1	2	3	4	5
11. Recognizes and addresses biased or inappropriate words, humor, gestures and behaviors in others and in our organizational communications.	1	2	3	4	5
12. Ensures that expectations of people are clear.	1	2	3	4	5
13. Creates a motivating environment for a variety of people, both individually and as a group.	1	2	3	4	5
14. Takes the biases of his/her own background into account when reviewing people's performance.	1	2	3	4	5
15. Gives others honest feedback (both positive and negative) on their performance in a manner appropriate to each individual's needs.	1	2	3	4	5
16. Turns over responsibility to people who are different from him/her as often as he/she does to people who are like him/her.	1	2	3	4	5
17. Shares unwritten rules with people who are different from him/her.	1	2	3	4	5
18. Keeps all people equally in the information and informal networking loop.	1	2	3	4	5
19. Fairly mediates conflicts when one person is similar to him/her and one is different.	1	2	3	4	5
20. Foresees situations with potential problems involving differences, and takes steps to prevent or defuse them.	1	2	3	4	5
21. Review the team's/organization's mission, strategies and goals to ensure that a diversity of views are included.	1	2	3	4	5
22. Actively looks for instances of structural inequality, and takes steps to correct them even if the issues are complex.	1	2	3	4	5

By: _____ **(due date) fax or send to:** _____.

You do not need to send the instruction letter, just this form.

Notes

Notes

Notes

Notes

Notes

Notes

Notes

Notes

Notes

Notes